From My Heart

Bonnie Hopman Reynolds

ISBN 978-1-63961-579-7 (paperback)
ISBN 978-1-63961-580-3 (digital)

Copyright © 2022 by Bonnie Hopman Reynolds

All rights reserved. No part of this publication may be reproduced, distributed, or transmitted in any form or by any means, including photocopying, recording, or other electronic or mechanical methods without the prior written permission of the publisher. For permission requests, solicit the publisher via the address below.

Christian Faith Publishing
832 Park Avenue
Meadville, PA 16335
www.christianfaithpublishing.com

Printed in the United States of America

To my beloved husband in heaven,
Rudolph Reynolds

Dear Rudy

Three long years have come and gone since the night you drifted away,
The pain of loss so acute back then, is with me yet today.
I've prayed so hard for God's help, just to get me through,
As I look back He did just that, in composing poems to you.
The aching that so consumed my heart, would swirl around in my mind,
I'd quickly grab a pen and paper, and write down every line.
I know not if you know or see, what's coming from my heart,
Writing gives me a feeling of connection, during this time that we're apart.
I have faith in scripture's promise, of together again we'll be,
But for now I'll keep on writing, till we meet for eternity.

A Widow's Lament

The loss of a spouse, be it husband or wife,
Is one of the hardest times, we face in this life.

Friends gather around, giving comfort and care,
Telling you how, they will always be there.

We put on a smile, try to not be forlorn,
Shed our tears in private, and silently mourn.

Another hurt suffered, at this time of transition,
Is the loss of our previous, social position.

The events we both enjoyed, so much before,
No longer occur, when you're a couple no more.

To go on a cruise, for a short getaway,
Requires a single person, for a double to pay.

Those shows watched and discussed, at night on TV,
Now there's no one to talk to, because there's just me.

The faraway dear friends, driving by so near,
Did not stop in, now that he is not here.

One cannot express the emptiness, of this once happy home,
The love within these walls can't be felt, sitting here alone.

Your whole life changes, nothing's the same,
That's how it is, no one's to blame.

Acceptance comes slowly, of this new life we're given,
But change we must do, as we continue on livin'.

I reflect on the good times, I'm so grateful for our life,
I do not like being a widow, I was happiest as his wife.

Acceptance

Will I ever see his picture, and accept he's here no more,
when someone's on the front porch, it's not him that's at the door.

When repairs are needed, his tools now lay and rust,
he is not here to fix things, a repairman is a must.

Shopping is a problem, always buying food for two,
not knowing how to cook for one, still making for him too.

There are shows and entertainment, we would like to see,
but do not want to go alone, he always went with me.

A feeling that he's just at work, it's hard to accept the fact,
the man whom I so dearly love, is never coming back.

Apollo

He was such an emaciated little guy, when to my home he came,
But still so sweet and loving, Apollo was his name.
He could not keep his food down, feeding was a chore,
So off to the vet for testing, to try and find a cure.
All is well health wise, for this precious little soul,
His eating problem solved, with just a puzzle bowl.
He's gaining weight now, and is happy as can be,
Playing with his squeaky toys and greeting company.
Now it's time for him to have, a family of his own,
To settle into a new life, in a loving, forever home.
Knowing he is doing well, and how great his life will be,
Is just what I had hoped for, tho he's taking a part of me.

Aunt Bess

I want to be like Aunt Bess, a kinder person you'll never find,
a mean or unkind act or thought, never crossed her mind.

She was my father's sister, and was such a blessing to me,
to have her gentle spirit, is all I could ever want to be.

A nurse at Millville hospital, newborns were in her care,
she lovingly tended to them, for the time that they were there.

Our son had food restrictions, no milk the doctor said,
by using potato water, she'd bake his yearned for bread.

There was huckleberry picking in the summer, it was just she and I,
and with the fruit we had gathered, she'd make me a berry pie.

The ravages of Alzheimer's, took her life away,
memories of the times we had, remain with me today.

Budley's Temptation

Four dog stockings were filled, and hung with great care,
But the temptation was just too great, for Budley to bear.

The toys are okay, and still remain intact,
However, for the treats, he just couldn't hold back.

All the cookies were consumed, when no one was around,
And only the treat wrappers, were left there to be found.

He has no remorse, nor feels any shame,
For our precious Budley, it was all just a game.

Chocolate-Covered Pretzels

Our nighttime dreams drift away, at the break of dawn,
upon our awakening, their memory is then gone.

Tho some may stay with us, for days and many a year,
and with a simple reminder, will once again appear.

I dreamt of chocolate pretzels, being rabid for a taste,
then just as I was about to eat one, my eyelids did awake.

It was such a disappointment, the yearning ran deep,
that hunger and memory, forever did I keep.

Returning years later, at a different place and time,
while at the chocolate candy store, waiting my turn in line.

As I perused all the goodies, and tempting candy display,
my eyes came to rest upon a case, with a small pretzel tray.

The dream coming back, a sign it was meant to be,
those luscious chocolate pretzels, were waiting there for me.

My taste buds were whetted, as the anticipation rose,
with the sweet chocolate aroma, drifting under my nose.

But fate stepped in alas, my hunger was for naught, when the man ahead said, "I'll take all the pretzels you've got".

Drats, no way I missed out again, I thought laughingly, my frustrating dream of years ago, was today a reality.

The China Virus

At the stroke of midnight, a new decade had begun,
    with folks celebrating 2020, and having so much fun.
January winter settled in, no omen it foretold,
    of the changes that were coming, far worse than the cold.
The first sign of trouble, ships quarantined at sea,
    no one could imagine the future, and how bad it would be.
The Wuhan pandemic, broke out and circled worldwide,
    no country was immune, there was no place to hide.
The frail and the elderly, were the victims hardest hit,
    as the death toll rose daily, there was no stopping it.
Schools quickly closed, students weren't learning in classrooms,
    thus a new way of teaching, and it's called virtual zoom.
Offices, businesses and sports events, all were closed down,
    the only merchants open, were the food stores in the towns.
Senior proms were cancelled, and graduation plans changed,
    in only months our lives had altered, and will never be the same.
Folks were confined to their homes, feeling like a house arrest,
    while some people felt it too restrictive, others felt it was for the best.
Rather than shopping for the latest fashion, our searches had to be,
    for needed supplies of face masks, gloves, and other PPE.
Spring turned into summer, and then into fall,
    COVID 19 was still rampant, and it affected all.
A pall was cast over the holidays, including Halloween,
    our only family contacts, were through a computer screen.
Then Trump made an announcement, vaccine shots had begun,
    giving us hope and encouragement for 2021.
This has been a road, we never traveled before,
    just hoping the vaccines are the answer, and be the ultimate cure.

Chris

It was a beautiful, sunny Easter morn,
so long ago when you were born.

As much as we wished your childhood to last,
Oh so rapidly those years did pass.

Too soon you became a man, fully grown,
and went off on adventures of your own.

Life is not easy as you have found,
it's a continuous seesaw of ups and downs.

The rough times you faced and struggled through,
made you stronger and we're so proud of you.

Your future looks bright with good things to come,
many years filled with happiness and then some.

We are so happy for you and want to convey,
our love and best wishes on your special birthday.

Christmas

Is it:
…twinkling lights appearing everywhere
…the scent of evergreens filling the air
…Yuletime carols playing in all the stores
…food and gifts being gathered for the poor
…selecting for loved ones the perfect gift
…children writing to Santa their wish lists
…ornaments brought out from years before
…holiday decorations adorning front doors
…some traditional fruitcakes aging in tins
…making batches of cookies to share with friends
…holiday cards from folks that we know
…boxing and mailing the packages to go
…families arriving from far away places
…with warm hugs for all and greeting new faces
…midnight church services with candles aglow
…a sermon from Luke and hymns that we know
…kitchens a bustle making delicious creations
…for the holiday feast for friends and relations

Is it a day, a week or Advent season,
or have we lost sight of the original reason?
The birth of a child, many centuries ago,
who grew into a man who loves us so.
He gave his life so that we may live,
and through him, God our sins will forgive.
So Christmas is actually every day of the year,
an eternal gift of forgiveness, because Jesus was here.
Merry Christmas to all and to all my best wishes.

Christmas 2020

We're facing an unwanted emotion, during the holiday season this year,
The dreaded Corona virus, has infected us with fear.
There'll be no warm embraces, nor kisses under mistletoe,
Instead we'll give out air hugs, and mmmwah kisses that we'll throw.
Twinkling trees and decorations, still we can behold,
But those festive fun filled gatherings, are being put on hold.
However there is something, that forever will never change,
It's the reason for the season, and Jesus is his name.
So on this challenging Christmas, when we wake up in the morn,
Let's be thankful for our blessings, and celebrate Christ was born.

Peace and blessing to all and to all Merry Christmas.

Class of '61
Millville High School

The ceremony was over and a new life had begun,
For the graduating seniors in the Class of '61.

Some were headed off to college, some struck out on their own,
As new adventures awaited them, with a great big world to roam

Careers, marriage and families have given them happiness, and
    maybe some strife,
As each one settled into their own, chosen niche in life.

Still the bonds formed so long ago, in those carefree high school days.
Remained with these classmates, friendships that time never fades.

Eagerly anticipated are the class reunions, held every five years.
Always glad to see one another, and remembering the departed with
    tears.

We know not our tomorrows, nor things of yet to come,
As life goes on and they continue to gather, the Class of '61.

Daddy's Girl

A wide-eyed moppet, with a crown full of curls,
captured your heart, she's your little girl.

Sesame Street, dancing and dress up play,
kept her so busy, day after day.

The days turned to months, and too soon into years,
can it be, her wedding day nears?

Just picturing her, as a beautiful bride,
sends chills up your spine, and brings tears to your eyes.

The vows are recited, they both say "I do",
for them it's a beginning, life starting anew.

Dogs

Dogs are fun, dogs are great,
I love dogs, they know no hate.

Zena

Such a sick and frightened little girl you were, with hardly any hair,
I said you're coming home with us and things will be better there.

All your troubles are behind you, we'll get you well again,
You'll have good food, a warm soft bed and a doctor to heal your pain.

But most of all we'll love you, and calm away your fears,
And hope you will forget the abuse, you've suffered over years.

The first few days were really rough, then things began to change,
The meds kicked in to treat your ills, that humans were to blame.

The time you came and gently laid, your head upon my knee,
I knew that I had passed your test, and you felt secure with me.

Your tail began to wag and wag, each day a faster pace,
And I could almost see a smile, upon that sweet, sweet face.

The weeks passed by and then the months, as you learned again to trust,
For you a forever home was found, and leaving us you must.

We knew the day would come, that we would finally part,
But precious Zena know that, you will forever remain in my heart.

Did You Ever

Did you ever feel snow falling, and sniff the clean crisp air?
Did you ever see a bucolic scene, and wish that you were there?

Did you ever encounter a thing so beautiful, it just made you cry?
Did you ever have such pain from grief, and asked "why did he die"?

Did you ever go on a ship at sea, and be lolled by the gentle waves?
Did you ever look at those unwanted pups, and wish each one you could save?

Did you ever listen to the rain, tapping on a roof of tin?
Did you ever buy a lottery ticket, and were sure that it would win?

Did you ever stand in a penthouse, and gaze at Central Park, blanketed in snow?
Did you ever fly in a copter, and been amazed at the world below?

Did you ever go on a balloon ride, and drift in a clear blue sky?
Did you ever see a homeless man, and asked what happened or why?

Did you ever go parasailing, over an ocean so crystal blue?
Did you ever feel befuddled, and wondered what will I do?

Did you ever witness a snow-capped Alp, peeking through a cloud from above?
Did you ever observe your sons being so kind, that it made you burst with love?

Our lives are filled with "did you evers", each person has his own,
A reflection of my experiences, as I ruminate in my chair alone.

Downtown Millville

Who ever imagined there would be no more,
Of that wonderful downtown of circa '64.
Grandpop would go for his plants and seed,
To Champions Hardware and Vanaman Feed.
A lady could always find the perfect dress,
At the Diana Shop, Prince's or Belle Godets.
Whatever a man's clothing size or style may be,
He had quite the choice at Frank's, Fath's or K&G.
The Children's Shop had clothes for tykes,
And carried a line called Merry Mites.
Endicott, Aronoff's and Freedman's, shoe stores in town,
Stocked many styles, sizes, and for kids, Buster Browns.
Colonial Shop and Fashion Shop had an array,
Of ladies accessories and lingerie.
Woolworth's and Newberry's at that time,
Were also called the five-and-dime.
Kids loved Grants and the Firestone Store,
Both loaded at Christmas with toys galore.
Millville National, City National and Millville Savings and Loan,
Were the places to go to finance your home.
When your "Doc" ordered an elixir, balm or pills,
Chiola's and Knowles your prescription would fill.
Broken watches then weren't thrown away,
Dave or Ted would repair them at O.K.
Decorator Studio and Dalton's had beautiful gifts,
To select for a bride from her registry list.
To Foster's and Harding's you went for the bling,

To purchase jewelry, watches and your wedding rings.
A variety of sofas, lamps, beds and so much more,
Could be found at Corson's and Ackerman's furniture stores.
For newspapers, magazines and all occasion cards,
One perused the aisles in McLaughlin's and Bozarth's.
Passing Belzer's and Abbott's one couldn't mistake,
The delightful aroma of bread, pies and cakes.
Grocery stores also were conveniently close by,
With the A&P and Acme being located on High.
Giuffra's made their own candy and sweets,
Many Easter baskets were full of their luscious treats.
To enjoy a dinner or late evening bite,
The Holly House was the place on a Friday night.
Jim's Lunch, Torelli's or Deluxe, 'twas a constant debate,
Over the burger sauce folks said had the best taste.
Social clubs did abound too, in this close knit region,
With the VFW, Elks, Eagles and American Legion.
And who can forget the Goody Shop,
The place to gather after a YMCA hop.
Doctors, lawyers and insurance companies too,
Were all right there on High to service you.
These are just some places that were on my list,
But there are so many more that I have missed.
This bustling town area had it all,
Before the outlets and shopping malls.
Life will never be the same as it was before,
Downtown in Millville in 1964.

Emptiness

How hollow is this place called home,
When you're living in it all alone.

The love and laughter that once did abound,
Is gone forever since you're not around.

I am thankful for all the years we had,
But I still can't help from feeling sad.

My happiest days were being your wife,
I'll love you forever, for the rest of my life.

Empty Arms

It's been a year since I held you, and watched you slip away,
Twelve months of loneliness and missing you, each and every day.
I yearn for the times you would hold me, and make everything alright.
Those evenings of us just relaxing, on a serene and peaceful night.
Your loving arms that would caress me, on a breezy night at sea,
Were the same strong and gentle ones that helped a rescue,
    that was frightened as could be.
Now all I have are my remembrances, of your kind and gentle ways,
And sadly those images are becoming, a blurred and fading haze.
My comfort now is to hug a pillow, made of the suits that you once wore,
And know you are in the arms of God, and suffering never more.

Endless Tears

The tears are with me every day,
They freely flow and won't go away.

I miss you so, all I do is cry,
Again I ask, why did you die?

Will the day ever come, again I'll smile,
I almost forgot how, it's been awhile.

Each day I simply sit and wait,
Till we meet again at the Pearly Gate.

Existing

Friends and family call each day,
"How're you doing," they will say.

My reply "Oh, I'm really doing well",
The truth to them I'll never tell.

Days come and go and I survive,
Feeling numb and half alive.

Our boys are what get me through,
I know they really miss you too.

I'll just go on and get things done,
And face each day as it may come.

I miss you so, Rudy.

Faith

There is a true reality, to things that we behold,
so many of our experiences, our hands cannot enfold.

Feeling of its existence, and knowing that it's there,
we cannot grab the wind, as it rustles through our hair.

We gaze upon the heavens, as clouds meander by,
one can't grasp the atmosphere, floating in the sky.

Springtime brings us flowers, and the fragrance of a rose,
but we're unable to capture the scent, drifting by our nose.

Sunshine brightens up the sky, at the early break of dawn,
rays cannot be gathered to use, when darkness comes upon.

Faith is an inner presence, a belief in my Lord I'll see,
and in His heaven He'll reunite, my precious Rudy and me.

Fall

The trees of Fall are changing, a beautiful sight to behold,
their green leaves of summer, have become a vibrant red and gold.

The days have a new crispness, you can feel it in the air,
signs of Halloween and Thanksgiving, are popping up everywhere.

Last of the fields are harvested, they lie barren as before,
late crops of yams and pumpkins, are now in every store.

For some of the sports minded, it's the favorite season of all,
especially for those fans, who love to play and watch football.

But alas the days grow colder, and the frost is on the ground,
the splendor of Fall is over, till next year rolls around.

Fred

It was at a homeless veterans stand down, where I first met Fred,
at night in a vacant field dugout, a bench became his cold bed.
This fellow had a family, two young children and a wife,
until his obsession for alcohol, consumed and ruined his life.
His only worldly possession, was a tool to open cans,
an addiction to hard liquor, had broken down this man.
While listening to his story, at my heart strings he did tug,
and he sobbed upon my shoulder, as I gave him a caring hug.
To many of the service agencies, his predicament he did share,
to help the homeless veterans, is the reason they all were there.
The next day was a special birthday, at 50 and alone he would be,
to show support and encouragement, I stopped by for him to see.
He then headed off to rehab, now it was all up to him,
to face his demonic problems, and work to be rid of them.
Weeks and many months passed by, there had been nary a word,
it was such a sweet surprise, when his voice on the phone I heard.
His life was back in order, and so very happy was he,
he spoke of his employment, and times with his family.
Life is not always easy, demonic challenges are harder than some,
Fred had the impetus and courage, his evil addiction to overcome.
The moral of the story, it's never too late to make amends,
you have control over your life, and how your day will end

Your Son

You watched your tiny little boy, grow up to be a man,
and as he stumbled along the way, you gently held his hand.

Now he takes another step, the biggest of his life,
as he vows to love that special person, who will soon become his wife.

Friendship

It was an ordinary trip for us, to the local food store,
to purchase our needed groceries, and nothing more.

As we talked, we thought for once, it really would be nice,
to buy something there, without first looking at the price.

We pondered just what that item, possibly could be,
knowing our very tight budgets, a stark reality.

Then the thought hit us, like a falling ton of bricks,
we knew what we could afford was, a box of TOOTHPICKS!

Scurrying to that aisle with carts, away we both went,
on achieving our mission, we were really hell-bent.

So many different kinds of them, was what we had found,
wood ones, frilly, square, plastic and even some were round.

The perfect one to choose for us, was an absolute must,
we laughed until we thought, our sides would surely bust.

We did what we had planned, and proud of ourselves were we,
for never once at the price, had we checked to see.

Over forty years, from that day, have long ago gone past,
and still so very fondly, that fun-filled memory lasts.

And becomes more precious over time, as we are growing old,
our friendship so precious way back then, today truly is pure gold.

So on her 75th birthday, the gift just had to be,
a solid gold toothpick, to my dear friend from me.

From Dad

I'll be with you always, son of mine,
and keep you close, all the time.

The shirts that I, no longer wear,
will be your reminder, I'm still there.

Although my face, you may not see,
remember, you're still a part of me.

I live on in you, my blood in your veins,
my heart, my soul and the Reynolds name.

God's Plan

Death has taken you from this earth, but not from within my heart,
I loved you so when you were here and continue, now that we're apart.

My love for you is eternal, for within my soul you'll remain,
it's God's plan when I will follow, and we'll be together again.

Good Night Sweetheart

Each night I lovingly kiss you, and wish that you were here.

Your ashes are a reminder, that you are ever near.

I know one day we'll unite again, in God's mansion up above,

For now I can only hold you in my heart, and profess my undying love.

Grandpop Joe

My memories of Grandpop Joe, go back to a time I was very young,
He was so kind and patient, we always had such fun.

His great big garden, was full of vegetables and flowers,
tending all those different plants, he worked for many hours.

In the Spring we'd go to Champion's, to purchase all his seeds,
He'd till the soil then plant fish heads, on which his crops would feed.

Early mornings would find him, sometimes at the break of dawn,
caring for his plants, hoeing the weeds as he went along.

As his crops began to produce, we'd carefully check each row,
to be sure to find ripe vegetables, searching vines both high and low.

Then with our baskets full, we'd head to the big oak tree,
and on that bench we'd husk and shell, just Grandpop Joe and me.

How delicious were those lunches, grandmom would prepare for us,
from our morning harvest, there was always more than enough.

I can see him still in the afternoons, taking a needed rest,
those special times with Grandpop Joe, were some of my childhoods
    best.

Grief

Grief is like a tunnel, with a light at the wrong end,
Instead of leading to a bright future, it shines on where you've been.

Halloween 2020

Ghosts and goblins at our door,
Kids we've never seen before.

Brings me back to years ago,
When all the "weeners" we did know.

Trying to guess each one's name,
And costume parties with spooky games.

Good times then and so much fun,
Bags full of treats for everyone.

Long gone are the years, since we were kids,
Our fearful haunt now, is the dreaded Covid.

Remember the rules and wear a mask,
Until this horrible virus has passed.

Wishing everyone from tots to teens,
A safe and Happy Halloween.

Happy Birthday Dad

On this day so long ago,
A babe was born whom we came to know,
As our father, so loving and kind,
A gentler man you will never find.

All too soon he left this life,
Behind to mourn, his children and wife.
Down the aisle, his daughters he could not walk,
Nor live to hear his grandsons talk.

But in our hearts he lives on today,
We miss you so Dad, Happy Birthday.

Happy Birthday Rudy

This year there'll be no birthday party,
for you born this day in 1940.

But today and always I'll celebrate,
your birth each year on the 28th.

I'm eternally grateful and forever will be.
that for a wife you chose me.

So at this time, dear husband of mine,
a toast to you of your favorite wine.

Salud and I miss you so much Rudy.

Hard Times

Sometimes life can be so harsh, it just makes you want to cry,
but I am ever so thankful, the Lord is on my side.

It's at those times when things are tough, and I don't know what to do,
I pray to God and ask his help, and he always leads me thru.

In Memory of Rudy Reynolds

December is coming to a close and his birthday is drawing near.
Things are terribly different now and my precious Rudy's not here.
No gifts, cards or birthday cake can be delivered to heaven above,
So I'm penning this tribute in memory of my buddy, my husband,
    my love.

It's Hard To Say Goodbye

We gathered at your bedside, fearing what lies ahead,
as all our dreams were shattered, by what the doctor said.

Your days on earth were numbered, there's nothing we could do,
your body was ravaged by a disease, that had overtaken you.

Options were very limited, you chose for Hospice care,
for the best relief from your pain, and the wonderful nurses there.

Each day we hugged and kissed, and held each other's hand,
overwhelmed by a feeling of helplessness, I couldn't save this man.

Words were hard to come by, I didn't know what to say,
while sitting by your bedside, as you were slowly slipping away.

Prayers were for your healing, oh please don't let him die,
repeating through tears I love you, I just couldn't say goodbye.

Just Us

The ceremony ended, and we were husband and wife,
Thus the journey began, into our newly married life,
        For Just us

Busy family times followed, with always so much to do,
For our quiet times together, I'd make a dinner for two,
        For Just us

Too soon our boys became men, and were off on their own,
Our house grew so quiet, when they moved from our home,
        It's Just us

Over the years we have traveled, so much did we see,
Sometimes with our friends, but mostly it would be,
        Only Just us

It all came to an end, on that horrible day,
When we listened to the words, the doc had to say,
        To Just us

Coming home from the hospital, was not to be,
Our years of just us, are now,
        Just me

Kindness

Kindness isn't expensive,
in fact it's actually free.
There is no money slot in the heart,
where you can pay a fee.
A gift from God to us,
implanted at our birth,
He provided us with living instructions,
when he put Jesus here on earth.
Be it man or beast, young or old,
if you should see a need,
Let kindness be your overwhelming guide,
and do that thoughtful deed.

Lava Larry

Lava Larry is there, to greet me every day,
when I open the back door, he doesn't run away.

He's a small gecko, living out in my backyard,
because he blends in so, seeing him is a little hard.

If you wonder how Lava Larry, ever got his name,
well, his color and the lava rocks, are just about the same.

I know it's always him, each time that I see,
missing a part of his tail, is a sure sign to me.

Sometimes such silly little things, that I see or do,
make my days a bit brighter, and bring on a smile or two.

I don't know how long Lava Larry, plans to stay around,
but until his tail grows back, he'll still be easily found.

Marriage is Like a Pair of Shoes

Marriage is like a pair of shoes. Not all pairs are the same style, color, size or will fit everyone's taste but, the right pair will last a long time.

New shoes may feel strange at first and after breaking in they give a little in spots to conform.

Both shoes are separate but they walk side by side throughout their lifespan; it would be difficult to walk over the sometimes rocky roads of life with only one shoe on, they need each other, they are a pair.

The older they get the more comfortable they become.

As with everything in life, time takes its toll; the leather becomes deeply creased and the soles begin to wear thin. Then the time comes where one is completely worn out and can no longer walk this earth, the other is left alone and is no longer part of what was a wonderful pair.

May Showers

Relaxing by the pool, with nary a soul around,
the low cooing of a dove, is such a restful sound.

The sun is brightly shining, as I slowly begin to tan,
being cooled by a gentle breeze, it's natures refreshing fan.

Then the clouds creep in, and darken up the sky,
I'll just sit and wait a while, hoping they'll pass by.

The serenity of the moment, interrupted by thunder's roar,
my peaceful time poolside, for today will be no more.

The scent of the fresh rainfall, ends my day in the sun,
there'll be more poolside days ahead, as summer's just begun.

Message to Rudy

May 30th again is upon us, it's approaching fast,
sadly it's a reminder, of four years since you passed.

Those hollow pangs of loss, are still with me every day,
and I thank God for our life, each night when I pray.

In all the fun-filled family times, and everything I do,
you're always in my thoughts, wishing you were there too.

Through the difficult times of past years, and especially now,
I miss your strength and comfort, but try to manage somehow.

Once more we'll be together, the time I know not when,
for now I cherish sweet memories, until we meet again.

Missing Gifts

Dear God, I know there will not be,
any gifts for Rudy, under my tree.

But neither is he suffering, anymore,
from the horrible pain, he had before.

On one hand I am grateful, he is with you,
however dear Lord, how I miss him too.

Missing Them

Its only been an hour since they left,
but feels like days ago.
Such happy times with the family here,
how I miss them when they go.
No more snuggles in the morning
with Chance jumping on my bed.
I'll miss those soft warm cuddles,
as he gently nuzzles my head.
The pet channel on TV is silent,
no need to turn it on.
Bode would sit intently and watch it,
but he too is gone.
Chris loves to watch football,
and sits in his father's chair.
That recliner is now vacant,
there's no one sitting there.
Valerie's special tree is dismantled,
and lies barren at the curb.
The guest room is eerily silent,
not a sound from there is heard.
But oh those beautiful memories,
of the time that they were here.
Flashbacks of those fun filled days remain,
and are so ever dear.

You

I look at the TV, and I see you,
I work at the computer, and see you there too.

In every part of our home, as I constantly look around,
vestiges that you're still here, can always be found.

Although it's been two years, since I touched your loving face,
the feeling of your presence, forever remains in this place.

Millville's Mike

Following the cold, dank days of winter, comes the freshness of a new spring,
to see the sleeping ground awaken, and hear little birdies sing.

As baseball season approaches, and the anticipation builds,
especially in South Jersey, for that player from Millville.

It's the beginning of Trout season, but fishing's not the game,
no, it's a major league member, and Trout is his last name.

When the Angels team is playing, local fans all gather around,
the TV's in their homes, or at local sports bars in the town.

Looking forward to this season, and more good games to come,
they remember those previous years, and plays that he has done.

They recall that moment, he's at bat with a 3-2 count,
and unlike mighty Casey, Millville's Mike does not strikeout.

He gave the bat a hearty swing, and watched it as it flew,
the ball soared high over the outfield, and disappeared from view.

As runners cross home plate, and add to the Angel's score,
Mike again is the team hero, he saved the game once more.

Now one may think the admiration, would all go to his head,
but Mike has remained so humble, and close to his hometown instead.

He's oh so young and talented, a brighter future still in sight,
no matter where that road my lead, he'll always be Millville's Mike.

Musings

I sit here musing on the beach, not a cloud in God's clear blue sky,
as folks in cars all search for parking, as they're slowly driving by.

People wading along the shore, others reading in their chairs,
while the aroma of lotion and hot dogs, drifts lazily through the air.

The perfect place to relax, and while away the day,
a peaceful time to gather thoughts, and to face what comes my way.

My Christmas Lament

The Santas are up and the trees are trimmed,
but nothing's the same, I am missing him.

The Christmas clock, that chimes each hour,
somehow has lost, its soothing power.

The gifts are wrapped, and ready to go,
to the friends and family, we love so.

None tagged Rudy, is the saddest part,
that he's not here, just breaks my heart.

My Christmas Wish

Santa, Santa, where can you be,
are you nearby and listening to me?

First, I'd ask for family and friends,
their good health and happiness will never end.

Then there's the lonely, sick and poor,
that their lives improve forevermore.

Hold all children of the world close to your heart,
your finest gifts to them impart.

And last but not least I beg of you,
for comfort to all and peace on earth too.

Dudley

He was such a little furry ball, when he came into our home,
weighing less than two pounds, he fit in one hand alone.

He had so many beds to choose from, but it would never fail,
we'd find him snuggled up and cozy, in Bentley's fluffy tail.

In his young and puppy stage, he was your typical little boy,
scattering things throughout the house, searching for a toy.

Later he became quite the comfort dog, for all rescued fosters here,
he'd help them feel at home, and calm away their fears.

Now at eighteen as he's gotten older, he's deaf and cannot see,
Dudley's still my little buddy and remains a comfort dog to me.

My Hometown

Life was so much fun in my hometown,
    good times with friends and close family around.
As I sat and reflected on that bygone time,
    a plethora of thoughts raced through my mind.
Walking to school each day, by way of Main Street,
    gathering friends as we went, that we would meet.
Snow days were special on that City Park hill,
    racing down on a sled, oh what a thrill!
Ice skating at the pond on a cold winter night,
    chatting with friends by the fire's flickering light.
Dances at night and activities by day,
    were fun times for the youth, at the YMCA.
At the Easter egg hunt, kids rushed for those sighted,
    with prizes and full baskets, they went home delighted.
Youth week parade culminated a host of events,
    on kids, pets and floats, much time had been spent.
When the circus came to town, what a sight to behold,
    the thrills and excitement, for both young and old.
Veterans were remembered for the sacrifices they made,
    honoring them at the Memorial Day parade.
Families gathered for picnics on the 4th of July,
    there were also boat races at a lake nearby.
Farms and gardens in the area did abound,
    and fresh produce stands could easily be found.
How good those veggie's tasted way back then,
    even our eggs were fresh, from local poultry farm hens.

Newly caught fish, crabs, clams and so much more,
    could be bought off the boat, with a ride to Yawp Shore.
Union Lake gave us respite from the summer heat,
    sunbathing, swimming and to Dix store for a treat.
To go to Camp Hollybrook was a kid's dream,
    with trips, activities and swims in the cold stream.
Sandlots were hives of activity too,
    a game could be played with many or a few.
Some games only ended when the streetlights came on,
    the field would be quiet till the next day did dawn.
Roller skates clamped to the sole of your shoe,
    the uneven sidewalks caused a spill or two.
Games of hopscotch, jump rope, hide-and-seek,
    were some of those played on East Main Street.
City Park tennis courts on a summer night,
    became a teen's dance floor under the lights.
Folks waited all year for this annual affair,
    the Mardi Gras attractions drew large crowds there.
A Halloween frolic was held at Culver School,
    a fun time was had by each goblin and ghoul.
Millville High School football had the best teams around,
    a win would result in a snake dance through town.
The Turkey Day game was an annual tradition,
    for a win and the coveted title, each player was wishin'.
Crowds gathered early on Christmas parade day,
    kids gave their letters to Santa along the way.
Christmas time on High Street was a beautiful sight,
    with seasonal music and the holiday lights.
Those days have long passed but forever will be,
    such wonderful hometown memories for me.

My Husband, My Buddy, My Life

It was at a 1957, Y dance, on the 23rd of November,
I met a 16-year-old fellow, that I'd forever remember,
as my husband, my buddy, my life.

After school and life events, too sundry to name,
it was on the 29th of September, when that man became,
my husband, my buddy, my life.

Added to our family, were two sons, Rudy and Chris,
life was full of activities, their games never missed,
with my husband, my buddy, my life.

A job move made us search, for a new neighborhood,
after looking at many places, we settled in Maplewood,
with my husband, my buddy, my life.

A wonderful place to live, meeting many new friends,
holiday parties and get togethers, the fun never ends,
with my husband, my buddy, my life.

Another job promotion, transferred us back to our town,
a house we designed and built, on a serene piece of ground,
with my husband, my buddy, my life.

Our boys became men, and struck out on their own,
which gave us the freedom, of this whole world to roam,
with my husband, my buddy, my life.

Life throws curveballs from time to time, ours was no exception,
unforeseen events resulted in, a change of our future direction,
with my husband, my buddy, my life.

After much thought and planning, moving to Florida it would be,
to a home in a warmer climate, near the beautiful blue sea,
with my husband, my buddy, my life.

We weren't there long when the cruise bug hit us, in full force,
fortunately, we settled on the coast, near many cruise ports,
with my husband, my buddy, my life.

Fifty-eight years later, we're still going strong,
happy and living the good life, as I plod along,
with my husband, my buddy, my life.

I am so grateful for you, and everything you have done,
and look forward to the tomorrows, that are yet to come,
with my husband, my buddy, my life.

Epilogue—May 30, 2017
My life is now empty, so sad but it's true,
our tomorrows are over, what will I do,
without my husband, my buddy, my life.

RIP my beloved Rudy.

My Sons

Grieve not for me when I'm not here,
Just touch your heart, I'm ever near.
I gave you life, I gave you breath,
We're never separated, even by death.
I loved you even before you were born,
Remember the good times, do not mourn.
My greatest wish for you would be,
To laugh and smile when you think of me.

New Year's Eve

It's 9:00 p.m. on December 31st,
in sixty years this is the worst.

I dread the passing of this year,
I've lost my Rudy and face eighteen with fear.

How will I go on, what will it be?
I need my Rudy right here with me.

We've always looked forward to the year anew,
now that he's gone, what will I do?

There's nothing to celebrate or reason to cheer,
because my precious Rudy, you're not here.

The Teachings of Only a Dog

What can a forlorn, odorous, filthy, tick-and-flea infested stray teach me
It's only a dog.

Having been so ill, Zena's extraordinary will to live taught me to
    never give up but
She's only a dog.

Mopar's gentle kiss on my cheek after being rescued from the shelter
    taught me how meaningful to another person an act of kindness
    may be but
He's only a dog.

Our senior lady Faith, exuded affection to everyone in the family
    showing that love is ageless and nondiscriminatory but
She's only a dog.

Sebastian's ability to overcome a severe leg injury and being left help-
    less in a canal to now being able to frolic in the pasture with the
    cows taught me to be persistent but
He's only a dog.

Baby's mourning at the loss of her family was evidence of her deep
    attachment and enlightened me to the unforeseen burdens oth-
    ers may be carrying but
She's only a dog.

Brady, having suffered years of being chained outdoors in all kinds of weather and the isolation by humans, still showered me with an abundance of affection and taught me about forgiveness but
He is only a dog.

Bogey's funny puppy antics taught me how good it feels to laugh more often but
He's only a dog.

Jake's voracious appetite and his penchant for raiding the food pantry taught me patience but
He's only a dog.

The timidness and shyness of Chance and being with him during a seizure taught me compassion for the fears and life-altering conditions endured by others but
He's only a dog.

These lessons were taught to me not by a book or in a classroom or by a professor but
Only by a dog.

Our Christmas Tree

Oh those wonderful Christmases, we had so very long ago,
to the deserted old rifle range, Dad and I would go.

We walked the woods in search of, that year's Christmas tree,
our quest to pick the perfect one, a cedar it would be.

He'd chop it down, we'd take it home, and put it up with care,
the top always bent at the ceiling, and its fragrance filled the air.

The strings of lights were checked, to be sure all were good,
because if one of them went out, then so all the others would.

Next ornaments were brought out, and carefully unwrapped,
some had special meaning, the memories they brought back.

Each strand of tinsel Dad would place, so meticulously,
with every piece hanging freely, as it dangled from the tree.

The magic of the season, too soon came to a close,
our beautiful tree dismantled, lying by the road.

But that's not the end of the story, for our Christmas tree,
as it celebrated Russian Christmas, in another home it would be.

Peace

My heart has such a painful ache, it's with me every day,
It's been there since you left, and will not go away.

I try to reflect on the good times, and how happy was our life,
I do not like being a widow, I so loved being your wife.

I thank the Lord for our life on earth, and for all that He has given,
My peace lies in knowing we'll be united again, in God's eternal heaven.

Reflecting on a Century of Changes

What if our forefathers of yore,
    could return to us for one day more.
Wonder what they would have to say,
    of the world we're living in today.
In their time, Millville centered around,
    the factories located in our town.
Wood's cotton mill is a thing of the past.
    they now own Wawa deli's that also sell gas.
For the elders I think, the worst would be,
    the total loss of the glass industry.
Whitall Tatum has been all torn down,
    there's nothing there but vacant ground.
At one time, Wheaton Glass did rate,
    as the largest family glass plant in the states.
Now the lehrs are down and the tanks have been drained,
    never to manufacture glass products again.
The ABCs they learned in the past,
    now stand for **A**ll **B**y **C**omputers, used in the class.
Gone are the operators, dial phones and such,
    calls now are made by voice commands and touch.
Those house calls, doctors can no longer do,
    you go to them, they don't come to you.
The trolley and Luna Park, they'd no longer see,
    beautiful homes are where the rides used to be.
The milkman and breadman don't deliver to your door,
    when those items are needed, it's off to the store.
Where laying out cash is no longer the way,

    most folks use credit or debit cards to pay.
Music on iTunes has surpassed,
    the need for records and phonographs.
Fancy tatted hankies lie idly in drawers,
    people use Kleenex, they're not needed anymore.
Men's suspenders and collars have gone by the way,
    as have women's corsets with whalebone stay.
Film development then was quite a process,
    now computers print photos, without all the mess.
The Millville Blues never could have imagined,
    the magnitude of Super Bowl and game day pageant.
The house where Mr. Thomas lived up on the hill,
    a city park and a tennis court there have been built.
The iceman and icehouse are both gone too,
    new refrigerators make all the ice for you.
The trusty old outhouse, long ago retired,
    is likely to meet its demise atop a bonfire.
Less canning of food is done today than before,
    processed food can be purchased at any grocery store.
Once, a family car was a real luxury,
    now it's quite common for households to have three.
Basement furnace coal bins are no longer there,
    the switch on the wall will give you heat or cool air.
Local door-to-door salesmen, making their rounds,
    with a case full of wares can no longer be found.
To our elder kinfolk, the most confusing might be,
    computers, keyless cars and a smart TV.
Were our ancestors happy living their simplistic way,
    or have advanced technologies made us happier today?
These innovations to us, are just an everyday thing,
    one has to wonder what the next century will bring.

Reflecting

You can't change yesterday, nor anything that's past,
tho many of those memories, will forever last.

Some recall the happy times, we wish we could relive,
but as for the hurtful ones, we must move on and forgive.

We know not our tomorrows, nor how many there will be,
hoping with anticipation, that a bright new day we'll see.

However there is a time we can control, and that is here today,
if we want to improve ourselves, in what we do and say.

If you are concerned about your life, and want to make amends,
there is no better time than now, before today's chance ends.

Reflection

We know not where our lives will lead, nor what God has in store,
no matter the number of our years on earth, we undoubtedly just
    want more.

There's always something to look forward to, an anticipated event.
We want to do and see everything, before all our days are spent.

We need to sit back and reflect, on all we've done and seen,
be thankful for our yesterdays and continue with our dreams.

Rudy Paul

Back in June of '64,
our family anxiously awaited for,
A special event that was to come,
the birth of you, our firstborn son.

At twelve after ten on a Saturday night,
you entered this world, what a beautiful sight.
This precious child for us to love,
a miracle that we daily, thank heaven above.

The happiness you gave from the very start,
brought smiles to our faces and joy to our hearts.
Many loved ones since, from this world had to go,
Nani, Uncle Frank, Mom mom, and Pop pop Joe.

They loved you so dearly, you brightened their days,
you constantly touch all of us, with your kind, thoughtful ways.
Thirty years have passed by in such a flash,
life moves along…sometimes too fast.

The love that began so very long ago,
has become more intense and continues to grow.
As you enter a new decade, our best wishes to you,
for good health and happiness, may your dreams all come true.

My Prayer

Dear Lord, I know not what to say, nor where I should start,
My precious Rudy has left me, and taken so much of my heart.

I thank Thee for the years we've had, how quickly they did pass,
Those oh so special times, I wish could forever last.

But in Your hands our lives are cast, and faith in You a must,
You know our tomorrows, and in You we place our trust.

Please dear Lord help me, thru the days of wild and murky seas,
Until that time we are reunited, my precious Rudy and me.

Amen.

Sam the Seagull

It was a sunny summer day, when Sam first appeared,
ambling down the marina dock, toward a man he did not fear.

He sat down right beside him, eyeing up his lunch,
that Sam was very hungry, the fellow had a hunch.

For Sam had a broken wing, and therefore could not fly,
he scavenged everywhere he could, in a struggle to survive.

So from that day forward, and till the season's end,
the worker brought some food, to feed his newfound friend.

After lunch was over, Sam would return as he had come,
looking for his next food source, and from whom he could bum.

One day Sam surprised his new friend, with an unexpected quirk,
he hopped up on his workbench, and watched him as he worked.

Soon came the cold months of winter, and the marina closed down,
there were no more dock lunches, and Sam could not be found.

With the approach of spring's warm weather, the business started anew,
while fondly remembering his lunchtime pal, Sam hobbled into view.

Days turned into months, and the friendship continued on,
Sam's walk became more labored, as he slowly moved along.

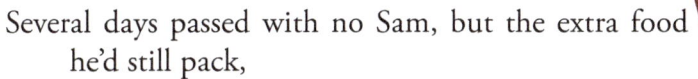

Several days passed with no Sam, but the extra food he'd still pack,
then finally came the time to accept, that Sam was not coming back.

Each day is a new experience, an unknown of with whom or how it will end,
he'll always have those memories, of the times spent with his feathered friend.

Saturday Night

It's Saturday night, and my furry boys are fine,
We're watching a rerun, of an old Dateline.
I look over to his chair, that is next to me,
In it is where Rudy, always would be.
As I reflect back, on the happy life we had,
It was so good then, but without him so sad.
I'd love to give, my sons a call,
But rather not bother, them at all.
I hope my boys, will never know,
The hurt of missing, a loved one so.
For you so blessed, to have your spouse there,
Reach out to them now, let them know you care.

Small Pleasures

On one of our visits to a homeless camp, Karen was waiting as I pulled up to our first stop. It was a hot, sultry summer day, and she quickly held the bottle of frozen water that I had given her to her flushed face. Pat, whose husband is wheelchair-bound back at their camp, came down the road with Terry and eagerly accepted her bottle that she held in both hands to hasten the melting process and get a cold drink.

The food truck arrived, as did our guests Ray, Wendy, Gary, "Doctor" Bob, and unnamed others. Lori took her bottle and wrapped it with the bottle of water she received with her meal to cool both. Tony's speech is difficult to understand at times, but his heartfelt "Thank you" came through loud and clear.

Each person only took a bottle until everyone had at least one, then they went back for seconds of the frozen water. It did not take long for the cooler to be emptied. Each and every one of them expressed their gratitude and appreciation with words and warm hugs.

Bucket, with his contagious smile, asked if he could have two. Bucket loves to fish and stays by the water but prefers to say he is camping and not homeless.

The food truck was packed up and ready to move to the next stop. As I walked toward my car, I spotted Gypsy, prancing and tail wagging wildly standing next to it; such a sweet girl. Is a dog still considered homeless if the owners shower her with the love and care she needs but live in a tent?

My lifetime experiences have far surpassed anything I could have conjured up in my childhood's wildest dreams, but one of the most treasured memories will always be of how the things we take for granted are not always available to everyone and the amount of pleasure you can give to someone with just a bottle of cold water.

Snowy Night

There is nothing more serene, than a snowy winter night,
as darkness gently rests upon the ground, covered in soft white.

Purest flakes of nature, have descended from the sky,
atop the barren earth of winter, a soft new coat doth lie.

There's such a welcomed crispness, drifting in the air,
the sight of trees wrapped cotton like, are a vision everywhere.

Daytime sounds are silenced, as the snow falls peacefully,
streets are now so vacant, slippery roads are traffic free.

The perfect time for a quiet walk, all the beauty to behold,
wearing our warm coats and hats, as a protection from the cold.

Too soon the nighttime passes, giving way to the next day's dawn,
and with it comes the melting sun, soon all the snow is gone.

How fondly those nights are remembered, their memory ne'er fades,
so grateful for those snowy nights, such fun in those younger days.

The Launch

In Florida, the excitement never ceases, on a NASA launch day,

Crowds gather along the east coast, to see a shuttle on its way.

Eyes are fixed on the horizon, searching for a rocket to rise in the sky,

And watch with awe and wonder, as the booster says its goodbye.

Carrying equipment and sometimes astronauts, with a massive outer space to explore,

It's off to new discoveries, on the moon, of Mars or more.

One cannot help but wonder, if the Wright brothers were here to see,

What their reactions to today's progress, from that first Kitty Hawk flight would be.

Spring Showers

Dark clouds are gathering, as a storm begins to brew,
the sun is disappearing, being hidden from earths view.

The dog can sense it in the air, and is quivering with fear,
a distant sound of thunder, foretells a storm is near.

Roaring booms grow louder, bright flashes light the sky,
and rain falls down upon the ground, still barren and so dry.

Spring showers are a signal for nature, to arouse her sleepy head,
as grass becomes a verdant green, flowers rise from their winter beds.

The days slowly grow longer, warm sunshine replaces the cold,
once drab landscapes are now covered, with flowers of pastel and gold.

Among the season pleasures, is to hear the birdies sing,
as we open our homes to welcome, the freshness of a new spring.

Spring

A new day is dawning, I hear the birdies sing,
they leave the cold of winter and return in the warmth of spring.

The big oak is waking, new leaf buds can be seen,
soon all its bare branches, will be wearing a coat of green.

The sleeping lawn that was covered, with a blanket of icy snow,
has awakened once again, and now begun to grow.

Tulips and other flowers, are raising their dormant heads,
It's time for them to rise and shine, from their protective beds.

There's nothing like the springtime air, it's so fresh and crystal clear.
A sign of the rebirth of nature, and a beautiful time of the year.

Summer

The school's dismissal bell rings, signaling the last day of the year,
the warm days of summer have arrived, vacation time is here.

Kids anxious to get to the seashore, to play in the waves and beach sand,
while parents relax and bask in the sunshine, working on their tans.

Baskets packed with picnic goodies, are opened up at noon,
as everyone gathers around them, their contents quickly consumed.

Still others head to camp sites, with their RV's and tents,
hoping to see those folks again, that in previous years they'd met.

The fun of roasting marshmallows, with friends by the campfires light,
and trying to catch lightening bugs, dancing in the dark of night.

The gentle summer showers, and the warmth from the sun above,
give life to the fresh fruits and vegetables, that we so dearly love.

Too soon the vacations are over, and the camping trips are done,
days are growing shorter, an omen of the seasons to come.

Memories of those carefree days, will forever linger on,
even after those days of summer, have long ago been gone.

Surviving

I never thought I could do it, exist two years without you,
however, with the help of God, I've been able to get through.

The days are so long and lonely, with a hollow feeling still there,
for comfort I hug your pillow and curl up in your chair.

So much has happened since you left, many of our friends are also gone,
Hans, Chris, Marco and precious Budley, also have passed on.

I am oh so thankful for our sons, and Dudley's always by my side,
but I do not want to burden them, they know not how much I've cried,

In my prayers I ask the Lord, to give you my everlasting love,
and I've had signs within my heart, I feel came from you above.

My life is in God's hands, his plan I do not know,
I'm at peace knowing you are pain free, but Rudy I miss you so.

Thank You

My TV was not working, no picture would appear,
Comcast said to take the parts, to a store that I was near.

On my way I saw parked, one of their Xfinity vans,
and stopped to talk to their compassionate, and helpful serviceman.

He checked the box, then the remote, and I really was in luck,
it was the remote that was broken, and he had a new one on his truck.

Now Rudy handled the electronics, and was the techie in our house,
mechanically I know nothing beyond, working with the mouse.

The man was kind and patient, as he walked me through the steps,
repeating numerous times to me, the installation and what is next.

I asked his name as I thanked him, for showing me what to do,
he said "my name is Rudy", I knew then, he'd been heaven-sent by you.

The Bride

I know that I will never see,
a lovelier bride than you will be.

The ceremony will start, the procession begins,
as the bridesmaids slowly, come marching in.

You'll follow in white, with the most beautiful smile,
and hold the arm of your father, as you walk down the aisle.

The groom beaming and nervous, is waiting ahead,
for rings to be exchanged, and vows to be said.

The reception that follows, is joyous and gay,
you could not have asked, for a more perfect day.

This event you have dreamed of, all of your life,
the time you and your loved one, become husband and wife.

The Chair

I sit here staring, but do not see,
your precious face, looking back at me.

The empty chair, just breaks my heart,
it's just so hard, now that we're apart.

On Sunday afternoons, you would be,
in that chair, watching sports TV.

That chair reminds me of the good times then,
and in it, you'll never sit again.

Dear Rudy, not a day goes by,
when I see that chair that I don't cry.

I miss you Rudy.

The Circus

In the early morning hours, before the break of dawn,
the caravan entered the city, and quietly moved along.

Curiosity rose with the morning sun, folks were drawn to the event,
and watched in awe and wonder, as the elephants raised the tent.

Is there anything we can do, excited children wanted to know,
and when they did they were rewarded, with free tickets to the show.

The tent was filled to capacity, not an empty seat was found,
anticipation filled the air, and excitement did abound.

The crowds emotions increased, as the conductor struck up band,
the parade of performers then marched by, waving to their fans.

And when the circus had ended, the crowd knew it was well worth,
the time and ticket price to see, the greatest show on earth.

A bit of Americana, remembered from days of yore,
the thrill of a circus coming to town, is dwindling more and more.

The Game

At home, the turkey is in the oven, and the pies are done,
The teams lined up on the field, a sign the game has begun.

A turkey day football game, played in rain, sleet and cold,
Is a Millville-Vineland school rivalry, over a century old.

The stadium is packed, each side with the cheering fans,
And music is resounding, from both the high school bands.

Players are psyched and ready, prepared to do their best,
To be the victorious winners, of this year's sports contest.

On the field there's lots of action, with so many passes and runs,
Where rough-fought yardage is gained, and penalties lose some.

The air of excitement increases, as the game nears the end,
With a score so very close, and a coveted title to defend.

And so it continues, as it has for so many years,
The anticipation again escalates, as the day is drawing near.

And when the game is over, its home for an abundant feast,
We thank the Lord for our blessings, and the food we're about to eat.

Enjoy this special time, with your family and friends,
Wishing all a Happy Thanksgiving, from beginning to the end.

The Lady

There was an elderly lady in my hometown, I'll not mention her by name,
Her Christmas tree at Easter time was not, her only claim to fame.

She was a free spirit, of clothes she'd had enough,
And shocked her church visitors, by greeting them in the buff.

Son's Day

Son's Day brings back sweet memories, of a chandelier and pink brush,

Send a message to my precious boys, on this special day I must.

I see a tall and lanky teen, walking down the street,

Carrying a large chandelier, dangling almost to his feet.

He's spent many an hour in the shop, so it would be just right,

A treasured gift from Rudy, was such a loving and beautiful sight.

Then there's the pink hair brush, always vanishing from my drawer,

I knew just where to look for it, in Chris' bath next door.

So when Chris got married, I knew what had to be,

The brush was the best gift I could give him, wrapped in love from me.

The Precious Neighbor

A gift from God moved in next door,
a tiny bundle to love and adore.

We knew you were special from the start,
you enthralled us all and captured our hearts.

Each day we eagerly looked forward to see,
what your new discovery or accomplishment would be.

As a rosebud opens into full bloom,
you grew from a child to an adult, all too soon.

So much of your life we were unable to share,
tho we moved away, we continue to care.

Such a kind and thoughtful person you've grown to be,
only the best for the future we can foresee.

At this hectic time when there's so much to do,
please know how much we all love you.

As through the hard times you must plod,
remember always, you're a gift from God.

The Raid

Listen folks, I've a story to tell,
Of a day in Millville that did not go well.
It was 1947, the fifteenth of March,
A usual Saturday with a peaceful start.
Families all busy, each one doing their thing,
Kids were playing and the adults were relaxing.
It was also a time some men gathered around,
A small gambling spot in the south end of town.
Now some Philly guys got wind of the place,
And headed to Millville for their share of the take.
Brandishing guns, they burst through the door,
Stole all the money and still wanted more.
The gamblers were dumbstruck and quite unaware,
That thugs from Philly would find them there.
With all the loot gathered they made a retreat,
To the get-away car and sped down the street.
The victims were furious and proceeded to chase,
The marauders around town at a frantic pace.
Bystanders were in awe as the cars careened by,
Disbelieving what was happening before their eyes.
To catch the thieves the pursuers were hell-bent,
But the crooks got away and back to Philly they went.
'Twas the beginning of the end of the games for these men,
A true tale of Millville that happened back then.

The Reflection

I see a face in the mirror, and wonder who can it be?
With all those lines and wrinkles, surely it can't be me.

As I ponder my reflection, the answer comes into view,
Some are worry lines of stressful times, that God has led me thru.

Others are the laugh lines, of a very blessed life,
With the antics of two young boys, and being Rudy's wife.

But I also see memorable journeys, along foreign streets and paths,
A road map of my life to date, is the reflection staring back.

The Seashore

How vivid are those memories, of family trips to the Jersey shore,
a place where once you visited, you always yearned for more.

Anticipation started mounting, with a whiff of the marshy air,
it's the first sign you're getting closer, and will very soon be there.

Our ride is almost over, the destination within our reach,
we anxiously await, a fun-filled day at the beach.

As the day was slipping by, and the sun about to set,
we headed for the boardwalk, our day not over yet.

Bright flashing lights of neon, lit up the nighttime sky,
while balmy summer breezes, cooled folks meandering by.

The rides were up and running, to our favorite one we'd go,
and from the top of the Ferris wheel, we'd wave to those below.

Enticing aromas engulfed us, as we walked along the boards,
we'd stop here and there for tasty bites, our appetite to reward.

Our day would finally end, and leave this place we must,
at that time there was no Disney, this was the happiest place to us.

The Spirit of Christmas

Christmas is a time of beautiful sights,
trees adorned with twinkle lights.

Festive wreaths hung on front doors,
decorated windows in all the stores.

Gaily wrapped gifts with ribbons tied,
smiling folks greeting passersby.

Donations made for the homeless and poor,
carolers singing and so much more.

If only the love and kindness that abound,
could be continued all year round.

Till Then

No one really knows my thoughts, and what's deep within my heart,
I'm just so sad and lonely, now that Rudy and I are apart.

I know he's in a better place, and all his pain is gone,
But I wish he were here with me, and a hug from him I long.

The sun comes up and sets each day, as I watch the time go by,
The dogs, my faithful companions, just sit and watch me cry.

I know the time will eventually come, when we'll be together again,
But all is by the grace of God, so I'll patiently wait until then.

True Friends

True friends are there in our darkest hour, when life is very bleak,
They're by our sides to comfort us, tho words they may not speak.

The bonds that formed so long ago, and nurtured in years gone by,
Are even stronger in our times of need, as they hug us while we cry.

One never knows tomorrow's fate, nor the journey that lies before,
However, true friendship is a priceless gift, that lasts forevermore.

Undying Love

It's been over a year since I kissed you, and you took your very last breath,
But nothing can weaken my love for you, not even the hand of death.

Your remains are always with me, never out of sight,
I kiss you and tell you I love you, each and every night.

Our home is now just a house, as vapid as can be,
Because you're not here with us, it's just the boys and me.

We've always been together, I feel now so alone,
There's a hollowness inside me, the likes I've never known.

We never know God's plan for us, or what he has in store,
But I cling to his promise that, we'll be together again forevermore.

Utopia

Palm fronds gently swaying, and sailboats passing by,
the sun is brightly shining, in a clear blue azure sky.

The gulls are loudly calling, I wonder what they say,
as they walk the sand in search of food, then finally fly away.

Waves are softly lapping, at the white and sandy shore,
washing over the empty shells, they deposited there before.

Children playing in the water, some folks are fast asleep,
a little bit of paradise, is spending a day at the beach.

Idle Time

I watch the cars as they drive by, wondering where they go,
is it shopping, work or a visit, to someone that I may know?

It really doesn't matter, it's certainly no business of mine,
however, it gives me something to do, a way of passing time.

Vagabond Boy

He was just a shaggy dog, whose family named him Boy,
he had a warm and loving home, but to wander was his joy.

Such a carefree happy pup, who made friends along the way,
sometimes he'd leave for hours, sometimes more than a day.

He roamed the city area, as if it was his big playground,
and on more than one occasion, in another city he was found.

Folks who saw him in far places, would stop and give Boy a ride,
when their car door would open, he'd quickly jump inside.

He'd sit up high on the back seat, as he was chauffeured home,
only for the next day, to be off again to roam.

He even had a police escort, the cops all knew him well,
if of those many adventures, Boy could only tell.

We

We met
(November 1957)

        We dated
        (5 years)

                We wed
                (September 29, 1962)

We laughed
(A lot)

        We loved
        (60 years)

                Now he's dead
                (May 30, 2017)

I sobbed
(Yesterday)

        I wept
        (Today)

                I'll cry
                (Tomorrow)

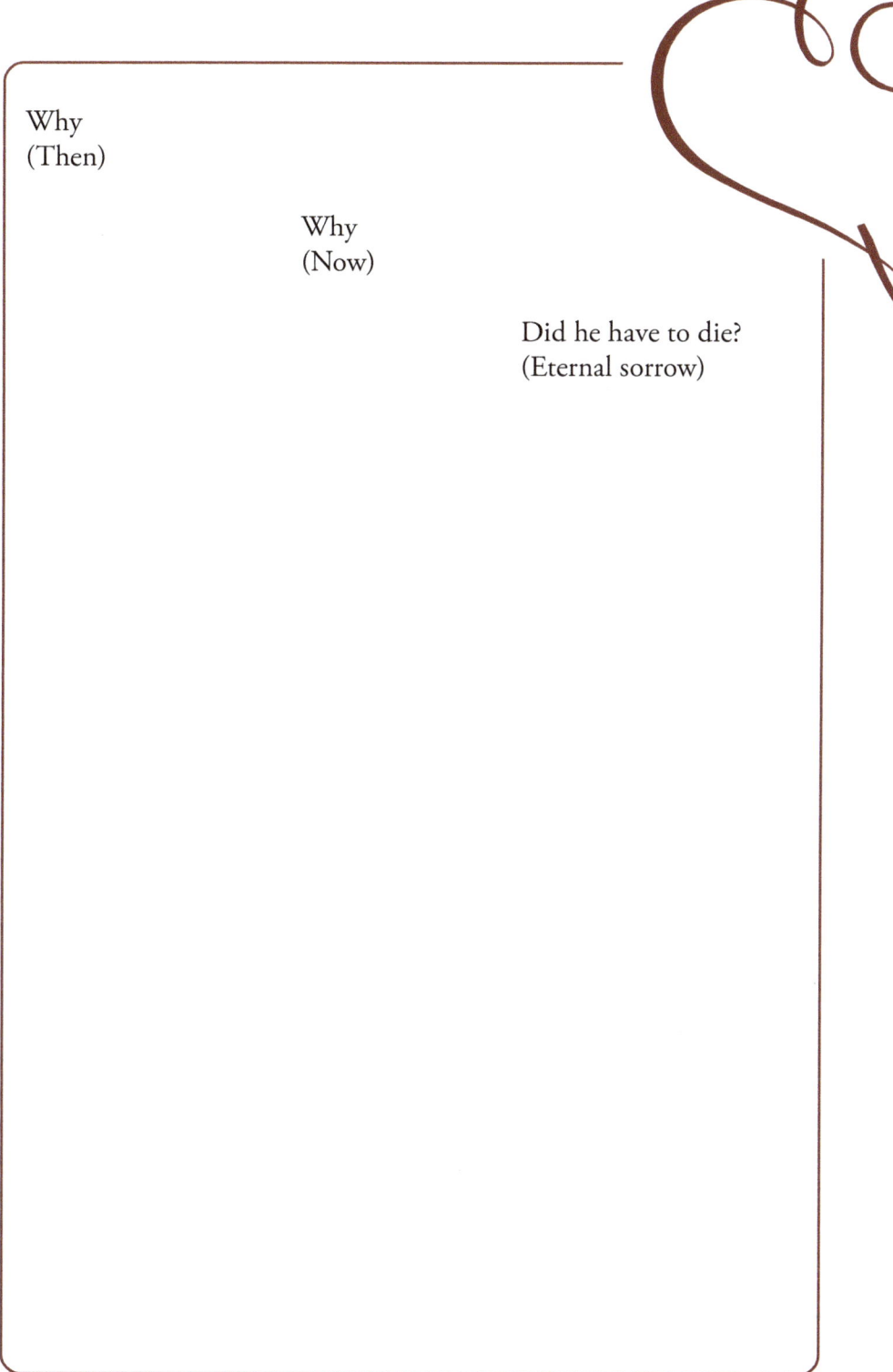

Why
(Then)

        Why
        (Now)

                Did he have to die?
                (Eternal sorrow)

Welcome Friends

If you're in the area, or would like to stop by for a chat,
Remember at my front door, there's always a welcome mat.

Tho my door may be shut tightly, there's a reason for the hinge,
It closes out the bleak weather, and opens for friends to come in.

No advance calls are ever needed, stop by anytime,
We'll have a cup of coffee, or perhaps a glass of wine.

Catch up on what's been happening, to whom, what and when,
It's so nice to have you visit, please come back again.

What Is Grief

Grief is:
...an empty recliner
...one place setting at the dinner table
...too much room in a king-size bed
...always having to drive yourself
...filing an individual tax return
...a half-empty walk-in closet
...calling a repairman to fix the screen door
...seeing the pressure washer gathering dust
...having to take the car for an oil change
...cooking for one person
...being on a cruise alone
...calling a computer geek
...only buying a bottle of one kind of wine
...decorating for Christmas
...May 30th, December 28th, and September 29th
...sitting next to a stranger on an airplane
...hugging a pillow
...a hollow feeling
...kissing a loved one's cremains good night

Always treasure the little things, you'll miss them when they're gone.

Why Oh Why

Why oh why did he have to die, will the day ever come I'll not grieve,
Please God can you tell me why, my Rudy this earth had to leave?

So many evil and malicious men, continue to live on,
While the kind and gentle ones, often are too soon gone.

I'm sorry if I'm selfish, and my ugly thoughts are coming through,
For in my heart I really know, Rudy is better dear God with you.

I wish I could rid this heart of mine, of the hurt and pain inside,
But only when we're together again, will my happiness be revived.

Why?

Another day, and you're not here,
As alone I sit, and wipe away my tears.

It's just so hard, for the boys and I,
Why did you get sick, and have to die.

Budley's head, rests upon my knee,
With eyes that ask, where can you be?

We miss you so, not a day goes by,
That I don't question, why, why, why?

Winter

The arctic winds are blowing, on a snowy winter night,
as I cozily sit here watching, the fires dancing light.

Not a soul is outside stirring, during this bone chilling time,
I pray all are safely in their homes, that're toasty warm like mine.

I snuggle into bed at night, soft blankets covering me,
so thankful for life's blessings, and a loving family.

My peaceful rest abruptly ends, when the kids jump out of bed,
with shouts "there's no school today", and scurry for their sleds.

They head for the highest hill, slipping all along the way,
to meet their friends who gather there, for a cold and fun filled day.

Too soon the sun begins to set, heading home they must go,
but always looking forward to tomorrow, and the next big winter snow.

Wishful Presents

Christmas is fast approaching, and there is so much to be done,
the tree to trim, gifts to wrap, before the family comes.

The stores are bustling with shoppers, as they wander thru the aisles,
searching for that perfect gift, that will make their loved one smile.

It's always been fun and exciting, in other years gone by,
to surf the web and department stores, selecting gifts for Rudy to buy,

But this year life is different, no gifts can he unwrap,
instead of looking for his presents, my eyes will be heaven cast.

About the Author

Bonnie Hopman Reynolds grew up and lived most of her life in New Jersey, where she and her husband Rudy raised two sons, Rudy and Chris. After the boys were out on their own, they decided to relocate to Florida.

With so many ports close by, they embarked on a new phase of their lives and entered the cruising and travel world.

Sadly, she lost her beloved Rudy, but those memories are a beautiful reminder of a grateful and blessed life.

CPSIA information can be obtained
at www.ICGtesting.com
Printed in the USA
BVHW020759190622
640129BV00020B/973